Whose Turn Is It?

Toyia Watkins-Bedeau

This book is a work of non-fiction. Unless otherwise noted, the author and the publisher make no explicit guarantees as to the accuracy of the information contained in this book and in some cases, names of people and places have been altered to protect their privacy.

Archway Publishing books may be ordered through booksellers or by contacting:

Archway Publishing
1663 Liberty Drive
Bloomington, IN 47403
www.archwaypublishing.com
1 (888) 242-5904

Scriptures taken from the King James Version of the Bible.

ISBN: 978-1-4808-6662-1 (sc)
ISBN: 978-1-4808-6664-5 (hc)
ISBN: 978-1-4808-6663-8 (e)

Print information available on the last page.

Archway Publishing rev. date: 10/03/2019

ARCHWAY
PUBLISHING

Train up a child in the way he should go:
and when he is old, he will not depart from it.

Proverbs 22:6

August 29, 1998

"Hey, guys, I need to go to the cleaners and retrieve some clothing," says Mom. "Let's go, please."

Takara, Olinette, and AJ come running from their rooms and rush toward the front door. AJ makes it first, then Olinette, then Takara. The three of them are scrambling to get the front door open. The door finally flies open, and Mom stands there watching them race toward the car.

They all rush to the passenger's side of Mom's car. Takara says, "It's my turn to sit in the front seat."

AJ says, No, it's my turn to sit in the front seat."

Olinette says, "No, it's my turn."

Mom walks to the car and looks, shaking her head. "Stop it," says Mom. "This is the third time this week that you three have been fighting about who will sit in the front seat."

The children all stop and stare at Mom.

"For right now I need all three of you to get in the back seat, please."

They slowly get in the back seat one by one. They buckle up, and Mom drives away.

The kids aren't talking while on their way to the cleaners, so mom initiates a conversation that sparks their interest. The chat lasts for the rest of the car ride to the cleaners. Mom asks, "Why do you think it's so hard for you guys to decide who will sit in the front seat? They begin to respond all at once, and Mom interrupts to say "one at a time, please." Olinette replies" "Maybe you should decide who will sit in the front seat Ma!"

"I think that you guys are big enough to decide, or work together to figure this out," says Mom. Each one voices their opinion, while the others listen, but no one comes up with a solution.

A few hours later, Mom makes another announcement that they will be going to the grocery store this time. The exact same thing happens again after the announcement. The three children once again race to the front door and are scrambling to get out. The door flies open, and once again it's a race to the car. They are pushing, shoving, laughing, and tussling while trying to get the car door open.

Mom rushes down the hallway and out the door to the car. "Stop it!" she yells. "Unbelievable! I will decide who will sit in the front seat. My goodness. Hmm …" She thinks for a moment. "Let's make it a race."

"A race?" they exclaim in the same voice.

"Yes, a race," says Mom. "I will walk about four houses down and stand next to the neighbor's mailbox. The first one to make it to me wins the race and gets to sit in the front seat." Mom walks four houses down, turns around, and says, "Stay on the road, try not to bump into each other, and don't rush toward me, please. I don't want anyone, including myself, getting hurt. Okay—on your mark, get set, go!"

They take off running, with every ounce of energy that they have, trying to win the race, while looking from the corner of their eyes to see who is winning. They are neck and neck until the very end. Then all of a sudden, Takara reaches the finish line one split second before her siblings, winning the race.

"Takara wins the competition!" says Mom.

Takara jumps up and down with excitement. She pumps her fists in the air and says, "Yes!" She is super excited. She knows that because she won the race, she will be the one to sit in the front seat today.

"Let's go, guys. It's getting late, and we still need to go to the grocery store," says Mom. Olinette and AJ jump in the back seat, and they are not happy.

AJ says, "Mom, we need a better solution to resolve this problem. It's not fair! Are you really going to want to referee a race every time we have to get into the car to go somewhere?"

Olinette nods her head in agreement. "Yeah, Ma, he's right."

"Okay," says Mom. "Give me a few days. I'll have to pray about it."

Mom backs out of the driveway, and off to the store they go. Takara looks back at her siblings with a superior smile and says, "Hey, look at the bright side—at least we each have our own window for the view."

"Whoopee!" says Olinette. "Let's give Takara a trophy."

Takara quickly replies, "Ah no! I get the trophy because I won the race, remember?"

Olinette attempts to respond, but Mom interrupts. "Okay, enough!"

AJ is laughing.

Mom looks in the rearview mirror at AJ and says, "Well, at least you're feeling better."

They finally arrive at the grocery store. Everyone gets out of the car and walks toward the store. They walk toward the shopping carts. Mom kneels down for two seconds to tie her shoelace, and then it starts, again . The children are struggling over the shopping cart .

AJ says, "It's my turn to push the cart."

Olinette says, "No, it's my turn to push it."

Takara says, "No, Oli. You pushed it last time; it's my turn to push it."

Mom looks on, once again shaking her head. People walking by are staring.

"Okay, this is embarrassing, and I need you guys to stop it right now. I will decide who will push the shopping cart. Whoever sits in the front seat will push the shopping cart for that day as well," Mom decides.

AJ stops and stares at Mom. "Really, Mom, it's not fair.! he exclaims, with disappointment on his face.

Olinette walks away with her hands folded and tears in her eyes.

Takara begins to push the cart with a big smile on her face. She is happy. Takara pushes the cart until they reach the last aisle. They pass the bakery just before checking out.

"Ma, may we have donuts from the bakery? They look fresh," Takara asks.

"Sure," says Mom.

They each grab a donut, and the baker gives Mom the UPC sticker to pay at check out. Mom places the label on her wrist so that she doesn't forget to pay at the register.

They walk toward the checkout area, as Mom is getting the final needed items. Everyone is quiet. After about a minute, they finally arrive at the checkout lanes. Everyone helps to put the items on the counter.

Mom says, "Thank you, guys; I appreciate you helping and working together." They check out and head back to the car.

Mom says, "Everyone help put the bags in the trunk, please." They all grab the bags and load them into the car. After packing the bags into the car, they all get in and buckle up. As Mom is putting the key in the ignition to start the car, she looks at the scanner on her wrist and realizes that she forgot to pay for the donuts. She exclaims, "Dang!"

"What happened, Mom?" asks AJ.

Mom holds her wrist up for the kids to see the sticker, and they all say at the same time, "You forgot to pay for the donuts."

"Yes, I did," Mom replies. "Let's go back and pay for them."

They unbuckle and walk back to the store. The kids take a seat in the waiting area, while Mom goes to pay. Mom looks for the shortest line and finds one that only has one person.

Mom walks up to the cashier and says, "I forgot to pay for these donuts."

The cashier scans the barcode, takes the money, gives Mom the receipt, and says, "Thank you."

"Let's go," says Mom. They walk back to the car, get in, buckle up, and Mom drives away.

On the way home, AJ asks Mom, "Why didn't you just keep the money? No one would ever know that you didn't pay for the donuts."

Mom smiles as she responds, "I'm so glad that you asked that question. It's called integrity. You have to do the right thing even when no one is looking. Taking something from a store without paying for it is stealing, and it's wrong. Never take anything that doesn't belong to you, okay?" Mom looks in the rearview mirror at Oli and AJ.

"Okay," they reply. After a few minutes, they arrive home.

Mom pulls into the driveway. As soon as she turns the car engine off, the children jump out of the car, leaving Mom to carry the bags in alone.

"Hey, kids, come back," says Mom. "Everyone come back, get a few bags, and take them inside. Thank you."

Everyone comes back, grabs the bags, and carries them inside. They go into the kitchen and place the bags on the counter. After they put the bags down, the kids head toward their rooms.

Mom says, "Oh, Takara! Can you help me put the groceries away, please?"

Olinette and AJ are tickled as Takara complains.

"Okay, Takara, you can't win them all," says Mom.

Soon it is dinnertime. The family sits at the dinner table. Mom asks Olinette to lead grace.

"Dear God, we thank you for this food that we are receiving for the nourishment of our bodies, in your name Jesus Amen."

After dinner, the kids place the dishes in the sink and head toward their rooms.

"Where are you guys going?" asks Mom. "You know the routine after dinner; that hasn't changed. What's wrong with you today?"

Olinette says, "Well, Mom, remember today is Takara's day, so we figured that she would be the one to help clean the kitchen."

Mom stops and just stares at Olinette for about five seconds. She begins to tap her feet and silently count to ten. This helps mom to stay calm. One, two, three, four, five, six, seven, eight, nine, ten.

Mom then takes a deep breath and replies, "you guys have always cleaned the kitchen together after dinner, remember? That way we get it done much faster."

They finish cleaning up in about six minutes. "See how quick that was?" says Mom.

After dinner and homework, it's time to shower and get ready for bed. The kids share a bathroom as their house has only two bathrooms, and the second one is in Mom's room. "It's time to shower," Mom says" "you guys can start now. Whose first"?

The three of them charge toward the bathroom all at once. Then all of a sudden, Aj and Olinette stops, turns looks at Mom and says, "Takara gets to shower first because she won the race right?"

"Ding, ding, ding! You are smart," says Mom. "You guys catch on fast. Do you think that you and Olinette can decide, without a fight, whose turn will be next?"

Takara starts laughing. She is laughing so much that Olinette, Mom, and AJ all stop and just stare at her for a minute. She is so tickled that there are tears coming from her eyes. After watching her laugh for a minute or so, they all begin to get amused as well. Soon everyone is laughing out of control. After everyone finally gains their composure, Takara takes her shower, while Olinette and AJ continue the debate on who is next. Mom suggests that they flip a coin to decide who will go next.

After everyone is done showering and ready for bed, AJ calls out, "Mom, we are ready for bed now, let's pray."

"Okay," Mom responds. "I'll be there in a minute." She meets them in the girls' room for prayer. "Okay, AJ, you lead the prayer tonight."

"Dear God, we thank you for bringing our family through another day, safely. Thank you for watching over us and protecting us. We thank you for our friends, family, church, and neighbors. Oh yes, and, God, please help Mom with a solution for all that we struggle with each day, especially whose turn it is to sit in the front seat. Please help her to make a decision that will be fair for everyone. Amen."

Mom then tucks them all in one by one, giving them the usual kiss good night. Mom's bedtime is also near. She finishes up a few things that she has to do before going to bed. She peeks in on the kids just before heading to bed. They are all fast asleep. Mom closes her room door and plops down on the bed as she takes a deep breath. *What a day this has been,* she says to herself. *God, only you have the answers, and I thank you in advance for the solution to every issue.* Mom lies down just to take a little power nap before her shower. She quickly falls fast asleep.

Suddenly, the alarm clock rings very loudly, directly into Mom's ear. It is 5:45 a.m. Mom jumps up. "Oh my," she says, "I fell asleep. I slept through the entire night. I must have been exhausted. I didn't even take a shower." Mom gets up and heads for the shower. After her shower, she sits on the bed and begins her morning prayer.

After her prayer, a still, small voice says, "Give the children an opportunity to pitch in ideas to help with the solution."

Mom walks toward the girls' room to wake them up. "Good morning, girls," she says as she enters their room first.

"Good morning, Mom," they reply with sleep in their voices.

Mom goes into AJ's room. "Morning, Jay."

"Morning, Mother," he replies as if he was already up.

"Okay, let's say our morning prayer."

The three of them respond at the same time. "Thank you, Jesus, for allowing us to live to see another day. In your name Jesus Amen."

Mom looks at them and just smiles. "I guess practice really does make perfect, huh?"

"I have an idea," says Mom. "I would like for each of you to try to think of something that could help us with the whose-turn-is-it issue."

Takara says, "Hey, I know the perfect solution. I should be the one to sit in the front seat because I am the oldest. How about that?"

Olinette responds, "No. I do believe that I get the best grades around here, so I should be the one to sit in the front seat. How about that?"

"Okay, kids, let's get ready; we only have about twenty-five minutes to get out of here, and it takes twenty or thirty minutes to get to Immokalee depending on traffic."

As usual, Mom counts down every five minutes or so until it's time to go.

"Ten minutes to go, guys; are you almost ready?"

AJ replies, "Yes, Mother."

Mom is done and pretty much ready to go as well. She is just finishing up with the final touches of her hair. "Make sure that all the rooms and bathroom lights are off, please," Says Mom.

All is quiet, and then it starts. They are at it again. The kids are scrambling to get the front door open, once again pushing and laughing as they struggle to get through.

Mom rushes down the hallway. "I cannot believe that you three are still at it."

By the time she gets to the living room, the front door flies open once again, and the kids are racing to the passenger's side of the car while Mom looks on in disbelief. Mom walks toward the car as they are tugging, pushing, pulling, and laughing, all in an attempt to get the car door open.

Then suddenly, AJ stops and says, "Wait! Mom, I have an idea."

Everyone stops in their tracks and stares at AJ. It is so quiet you could hear a pin drop in the grass.

AJ begins to point.

He starts with Olinette, then Takara, then himself. As he points at the girls and himself, he says a day. Today is Tuesday, so he begins with Tuesday, Wednesday, Thursday, Friday, Saturday, and then Sunday. He begins to explain, "There are seven days in a week, and there are three of us. It will work like this. Two of us will get to sit in the front seat at least two days out of the week. The one day that is left, Monday, everyone will have to sit in the back seat for now, and as Mom has said, whoever sits in the front seat gets to do all the other things as well, like pushing the cart and showering first. Mom, you can even use Monday as an incentive for good report cards. Whoever gets the best report card going forward will sit in the front seat on Mondays. "What do you guys think?" AJ asks.

Everyone agrees that it is a good idea and will give it a try. The current day is Tuesday, so it's Olinette's day to sit in the front. She happily jumps into the front seat with a big smile.

AJ and Takara get in the back with no problem. Everyone buckles up, and Mom drives away.

Mom wants to be clear about the days, so she asks everyone beginning with Olinette, "What are your two days?"

Olinette replies, "Tuesday and Friday."

"Takara, what are your two days?"

Takara replies, "Sunday and Thursday."

"AJ, what are your two days?"

He answers, "Wednesday and Saturday."

"Okay, great; don't forget your days."

All is great as the rest of the week seems to fly by quickly and smoothly, with no fighting at all. Everyone is happy, and the new arrangement is working great.

Mom gets into her car after leaving work on Friday. She pauses before starting the car. She looks up toward the sky and says, "Thank you, Lord, for answering our prayers. You are indeed an awesome God."

The weekend flies by, and Monday morning comes, quickly. Everyone is doing their usual morning chores and preparing for the day ahead. Mom is doing her usual countdown as she, and the kids are preparing to leave for work and school. Two minutes before they are out, Mom reminds them to make sure that all the lights are off. The kids quietly head outside and walk to the car. They all get in the back seat.

Mom gets in the car, turns around, looks in the back seat, and asks, "Whose turn is it to sit in the front seat?"

They all reply in the same voice at the same time, "Nobody's!"

"I totally forgot," says Mom. Everyone laughs. From that day forward, there are no more questions about whose turn it is to sit in the front seat.

Printed in the United States
By Bookmasters